Ladyb

Ladybird

A bumblebee was buzzing
around a flower
when a ladybird flew by.

"Why are you flying
so fast, Ladybird?"
asked Bumblebee.

"My house is on fire
and my children
are home," said Ladybird.
"A little girl told me."

"I'll come with you,"
said Bumblebee.

A butterfly was fluttering on a leaf when Ladybird and Bumblebee flew by.

"Why are you flying so fast, Bumblebee?" asked Butterfly.

"Ladybird's house is on fire and her children are home," said Bumblebee. "A little girl told her."

"I'll come with you," said Butterfly.

A dragonfly was hovering
over the water
when Ladybird, Bumblebee,
and Butterfly flew by.

"Why are you flying
so fast, Butterfly?"
asked Dragonfly.

"Ladybird's house
is on fire and her children
are home," said Butterfly.
"A little girl told her."

"I'll come with you,"
said Dragonfly.

Ladybird's house
was on fire.

"Help! Help! Help!"
cried the three
little ladybirds.
"We can't find
our way out!
The smoke is
too thick!"

Ladybird cried.
Butterfly cried.
Dragonfly cried.

But Bumblebee
went up to the fire,
buzzing and buzzing...

"Keep down on
your knees-z-z-z-Z-Z
if you please-z-z-z-Z-Z
and come to my
buzz-z-z-z-Z-Z!"

The three little ladybirds
came towards
Bumblebee's buzz.
They came out
of the burning house.

"Thank you, Bumblebee,"
said Ladybird.
"Now let's all go
down to the pond.
The cold water
will do us good!"

Ladybird, ladybird,
Fly away home.
Your house is on fire
And your children are gone,
All but one,
And her name is Ann,
And she crept under
The pudding pan.

Bed, Ben! Bed!

Ali
shed
Ben
Pen
hut

tent
Dad
Spot
Rob
bed
Kim
Tim

Ben! Ben!

Bed, Ben... bed!

Is it Ben?
Is it Ben in the hut?

No, it is Rob and Spot
in the hut.

Dad went to the tent.

Is it Ben?

Is it Ben in the tent?

No, it is Pen and Kim
in the tent.

Dad went to the shed.

Is it Ben?
Is it Ben in the shed?

No, it is Ali and Tim
in the shed.

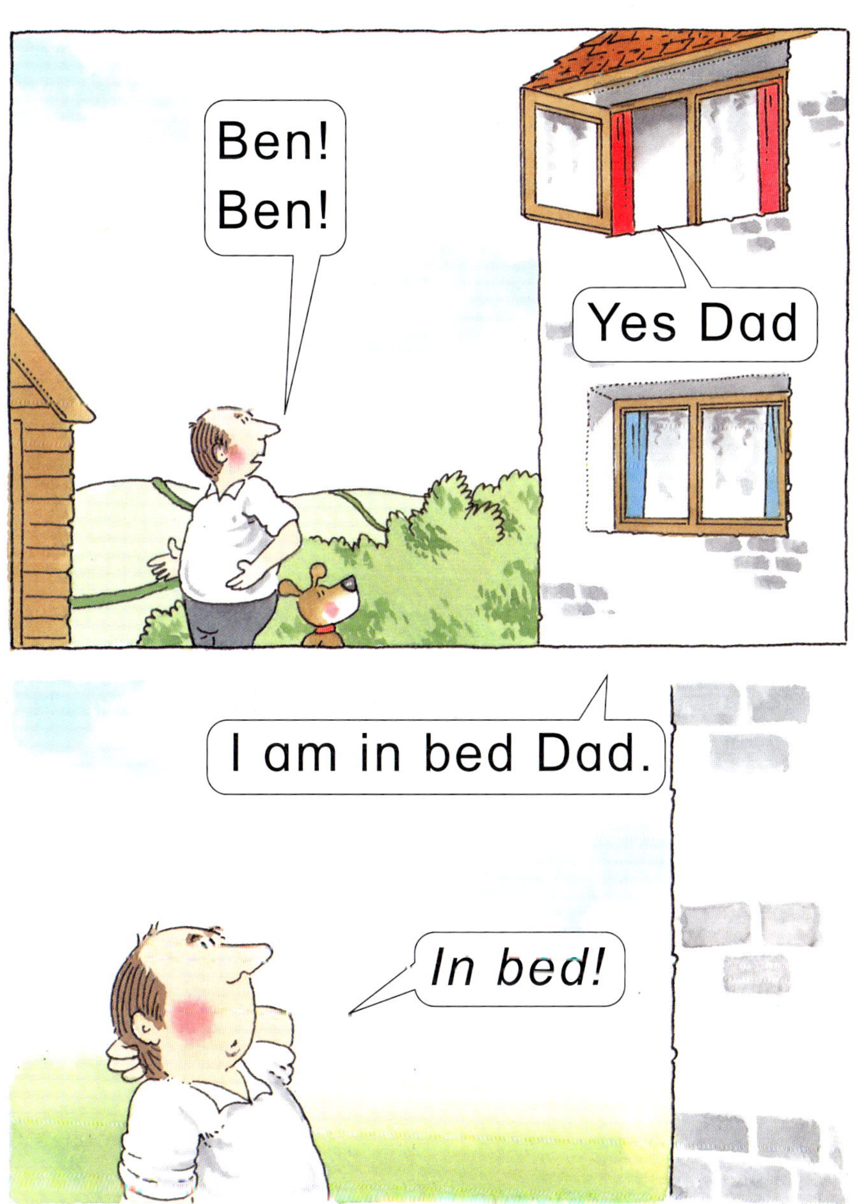

Ben!
Ben!
Yes Dad
I am in bed Dad.
In bed!

Yes, Ben is in bed!

Ben is in bed.
Ben likes it in bed!

Mum ran and ran

hut
pug

Ben
Pen
Dad
Mum

Pen is in the hut.

Ben is in the hut.

Bang!
Bang!
Mum! Mum!

Mum,
can we
help?

Pen helps Mum,

and Dad and Ben help.

Mum went.

Mum ran

and ran

and

ran!

Dad ran. Pen ran. Ben ran.

The pug

ran

and ran.

Down
down
down

Down it went!

Get up
Ali.
Get up.

Pen and Ben and Mum!